Wilts & Dorset Recollections

Chris Harris

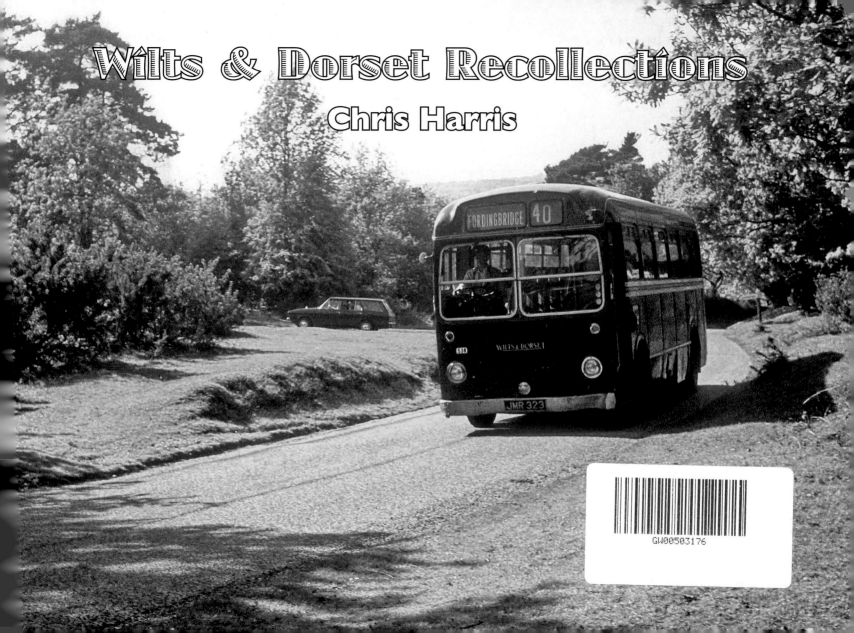

Contents

About the author

First published in 2016

British Library Cataloguing in Publication Data

A catalogue record for this book is available from the British Library.

ISBN 978 1 85794 494 5

Silver Link Publishing Ltd
The Trundle
Ringstead Road
Great Addington
Kettering
Northants NN14 4BW

Tel/Fax: 01536 330588
email: sales@nostalgiacollection.com
Website: www.nostalgiacollection.com

Printed and bound in the Czech Republic

Front cover: **SALISBURY** This evocative photograph of Salisbury bus station in the mid-1960s will bring back many happy memories. Closest to the camera on the right, Bristol LS5G saloon NAM 117, new to Wilts & Dorset in December 1955, is ready to operate to Fordingbridge on route 40, while passengers can be seen boarding similar vehicle NHR 128, which dated from 1956, for the journey on route 1 via the Woodford valley to Amesbury. Also in the photograph, a Bristol FS double-decker (behind NAM 117) will shortly depart on service 709 to Swindon, while a Bristol LD is marked up for the 38 route to Bournemouth. *H&DW&D Heritage Collection, courtesy Peter Cook*

Chris Harris spent his career in the bus industry, having joined Hants & Dorset Motor Services as a conductor at Poole depot back in the days when that Company's buses were still painted in Tilling Green livery. After some years on the road he was seconded to the Market Analysis Project in 1978, and later worked in Hants & Dorset's publicity department until that Company was broken up in 1983. He then joined the Wilts & Dorset Bus Company, becoming marketing assistant in 1986 and head of marketing in January 1993.

Chris remained head of marketing when the Go-Ahead Group bought Wilts & Dorset in 2003 and subsequently became Public Relations Manager for the Go South Coast family of companies in 2007; he remained in this position until his retirement a few years ago.

Since 1999 Chris has written a number of books covering transport history and local history, and derives great pleasure and satisfaction in doing so. Other interests and pleasures include walking in the countryside, literature and classical music. In retirement Chris still edits the Go South Coast staff magazine, and also edits *Wessex Review* for the Wessex Transport Society.

Title page: **WOODGREEN** Epitomising Wilts & Dorset's rural routes during the 1950s and 1960s, dual-purpose Bristol LS6G saloon JME 323, new in 1953, was photographed in attractive surroundings at Woodgreen while operating route 40 to Fordingbridge in May 1970. *Omnicolour*

Rear cover: **HINDON** A feature of Wilts & Dorset's operations was the number of outstations at which vehicles and crews were based. Seen at Hindon outstation in 1972 is lowbridge-bodied Bristol KSW6B JWV 263, which had operated from Salisbury via Wilton and Dinton on route 25. *Brian Jackson*

Foreword

This excellent book illustrates and explains the history of our Company, from the very early days of bus operation in 1915 through to the familiar buses on our roads in the present day.

The Company has faced many challenges and seen very many changes over the years. These include regulation, deregulation, nationalisation and privatisation. We also experienced the dark years of the Second World War, when tragically some of our employees gave their lives in active service.

Technology has changed hugely since 1915, and the pioneers from those early days would be amazed at our current state-of-the-art vehicles, ticketing and on-line presence. However, the basic objectives of the business would be instantly recognisable to them – providing safe, attractive and economical transport throughout our area throughout the year.

This book richly illustrates the huge variety of buses and coaches we have used over the years. Of course, it is our employee team that has kept the wheels turning in this time. They did, and still do, an amazing job at all times of the day and in all weathers to keep services running.

Enjoy this book, and then come and enjoy the real thing. Nothing beats the views of our beautiful coast and countryside, enjoyed from the top of a bus.

Andrew Wickham
Managing Director, Go South Coast
Poole, Dorset
October 2016

Introduction

The history of the excellent Salisbury Reds network of buses in Wiltshire can be traced back to when Edwin Maurice Coombes started a bus service between Amesbury and Salisbury in August 1914, which led to Wilts & Dorset Motor Services Limited being registered at Companies House on 4 January 1915. The Company traded as Wilts & Dorset until 1972, when it was subsumed into Hants & Dorset whilst in the ownership of the National Bus Company. Eleven years later the National Bus Company decided to break up the larger operating companies into smaller units, and thus the Wilts & Dorset Bus Company came into being from April 1983, albeit with a somewhat different operating area than the previous Wilts & Dorset Motor Services.

Some people have expressed the view that the Wilts & Dorset Bus Company registered in 1983 was a completely separate entity from Wilts & Dorset Motor Services registered in 1915. It is true that they have different company registration numbers, but on the other hand there are loyal long-serving members of staff who have worked for Wilts & Dorset Motor Services, Hants & Dorset and the Wilts & Dorset Bus Company – all without changing their place of work or job description. As far as the customer was concerned, the same cheerful, helpful and friendly people were doing the same jobs, and given that for the majority of people the identity of the Company is derived from the people and the services offered rather than a number on a certificate in an office somewhere, I think there is little harm in treating the history as continuous from 1915 to 2016.

In this book you will find a wealth of photographs, with detailed and informative captions, that will give a real flavour of the Company during the past 101 years. I was lucky enough to spend my working life in the bus industry, joining Hants & Dorset as a conductor at Poole depot back in the days when that Company's buses were still painted green, then joining the Wilts & Dorset Bus Company when Hants & Dorset was split into smaller units in 1983 – see 'About the author' on the opposite page. I have therefore been privileged to have taken an active part in some of the events and developments described in this book.

I would like to warmly thank everyone who has helped make the production of this book possible. David Pennels, Peter Cook, Brian Jackson, John Weager and Chris Aston have all very kindly made photographs available from their collections, and have also helped with valuable information. Peter Cook has loaned photographs from the Hants & Dorset Wilts & Dorset Heritage Collection together with some that he had taken himself. David Pennels, the Kithead Trust and the Wiltshire History Centre have kindly provided many details that have greatly enriched this book. Technical help from Brian Jackson and Donna Vincent has been much appreciated, and particular thanks to Andrew Wickham for kindly providing the Foreword. I would also especially like to thank Peter Townsend and Will Adams of The Nostalgia Collection for their kindness, help and support.

Of course, in a book of this size it has not been possible to write a complete and detailed history of the Company, but if you would like more information, my book *A Century of Service; the year by year story of Wilts & Dorset 1915-2015*, published by Best Impressions in 2015, sets out the story on a year-by-year basis in great detail.

I hope you will find the photographs and information in *Wilts & Dorset Recollections* to be of great interest – and many may prompt happy memories and reminiscences. I hope you will enjoy reading this book as much as I have enjoyed writing it.

Chris Harris
Poole, Dorset   October 2016

SALISBURY Wilts & Dorset Motor Services Limited was registered at Companies House, London, on 4 January 1915. Six of the first seven vehicles purchased by the Company featured locally-built Scout chassis. IB 802, seen here in Salisbury's Guildhall Square, was bought new by Wilts & Dorset in March 1915; this 37hp Scout vehicle carried a charabanc body that was also locally built – by Marks of Wilton. This vehicle was withdrawn from the fleet in 1917, by the end of which year Wilts & Dorset was at a low ebb, operating just one bus on one route. Nonetheless, the Company survived the difficulties caused by the First World War, although the Salisbury-based Scout Motors did not. The Government requisitioned the machinery owned by Scout for the war effort; production was not able to resume until 1920, and Scout Motors was wound up in 1921. Wilts & Dorset only operated Scout vehicles for a short time, but it is true to say that it was the local Scout product that first put Wilts & Dorset on the road as a bus operator. *David Pennels collection*

SALISBURY Wilts & Dorset acquired this 40hp McCurd bus, IB 806, in August 1916; it set an important historic precedent, being the first of the Company's vehicles to be painted red – the earlier vehicles had carried a yellow livery. The body fitted to this McCurd bus was second-hand, having previously been carried by a Southend-on-Sea Corporation Tilling Stevens; it had a rear entrance and perimeter seating for 26 passengers. This was the one vehicle retained by the Company to work the route between Salisbury and Amesbury via the Woodford valley in 1917. In fact, IB 806 proved to be an excellent investment for Wilts & Dorset, remaining in the fleet until 1926, when it was sold for £85; it subsequently saw further service with Jeanes of Weymouth before its final use as a garden summerhouse at Chickerell. *David Pennels collection*

Right: **ON THE A338** Wilts & Dorset commenced a route from Salisbury to Bournemouth via Downton, Fordingbridge, Ringwood and Christchurch in 1920. Seen operating on the route is CD 3177, an AEC YC that was bought new by Wilts & Dorset in April 1920. It carries a 35-seat rear-entrance bus body by Dodson. CD 3177 was in service with Wilts & Dorset until September 1929. *Brian Jackson collection*

Left: **SALISBURY** The first double-deck bus to join the Wilts & Dorset fleet entered service in July 1919. An AEC YC, CD 2555 carried an open-top double-deck body by Brush, with seats for 45 passengers. This view illustrates the open staircase and rear platform; whilst a ride on the upper deck was no doubt quite enjoyable on a fine summer day, it would have been distinctly less pleasant during the winter months when all but the most hardy smokers would probably have made for the lower-deck seats that offered more protection from the elements. Notice the large advertisement for Style & Gerrish on the rear of the upper deck; this department store in Blue Boar Row, Salisbury, trades as Debenham's in the 21st century. CD 2555 was withdrawn from service in December 1929, and the AEC chassis saw further use as a lorry in Kent. *Brian Jackson collection*

Right: **WILTON** When CD 3330 first entered service with Wilts & Dorset in 1919 it had been fitted with a second-hand 31-seat charabanc body by Harrington. However, this AEC YC was rebodied as a double-deck bus early in 1921, using a second-hand Dodson body that had originally been carried by a London General Omnibus Company vehicle. CD 3330 is seen operating as a double-decker on the Salisbury to Wilton route, with the crew of driver and conductor standing proudly alongside. CD 3330 was withdrawn in December 1929. *David Pennels collection*

Below: **SALISBURY** When Wilts & Dorset was first established in 1915, the Company's registered office had been at 46 High Street, Amesbury; this was moved to 2 St Thomas's Square, Salisbury, from 5 February 1917. Three Wilts & Dorset vehicles are seen outside the St Thomas's Square premises in 1928. On the left and in the centre we see two Leylands, MR 6636 and MR 6437, dating from 1926, while on the right of the group is MW 1854, a Dennis that had been new in 1928. Notice the traditional way of advertising coach excursions on chalk boards propped against the vehicles. There are some tempting excursions on offer including Lyndhurst, Sandbanks and Bognor Regis. The board on the extreme right advertises daily trips to Stonehenge — the first beginnings of the very successful Stonehenge Tour that operates in the 21st century. *David Pennels collection*

Right: **ANDOVER** In late 1929 Wilts & Dorset started a network of four cross-town routes in Andover, based on a town-centre terminus at the Guildhall. Leyland TD1 MW 7051 was new to Wilts & Dorset in July 1930, and was photographed on a bright winter's day while operating on the Andover town routes. It carries a 48-seat lowbridge double-deck body, also built by Leyland. For the next 23 years, the vast majority of double-deck buses taken into the Wilts & Dorset fleet would be fitted with lowbridge bodywork; as their name implies, these buses had a reduced overall height, achieved by having a sunken side gangway along the offside of the upper deck, with passengers sitting in rows of four. Many people felt that this layout was less than ideal, but full-height buses with a central gangway on both decks were too high to pass beneath a number of railway bridges and other overhead obstructions in the Wilts & Dorset area. MW 7051 was in service with the Company until April 1952. *Arthur Blake, David Pennels collection*

Below: **WEYMOUTH** It was also in 1929 that Wilts & Dorset started a route from Salisbury to Weymouth via Blandford and Dorchester. When the route commenced, Southern National declined Wilts & Dorset's offer of a joint service. Five years later in 1934 Southern National approached Wilts & Dorset with a proposal for a joint service on a 50/50 basis, but having invested significantly

in the development of the route, Wilts & Dorset declined this proposition. It was not until January 1949 that this became a joint Wilts & Dorset and Southern National route. Here we see a very unfortunate incident that took place on 9 July 1936; Leyland TD4 WV 7474, new in July 1935, has overturned at Ridgeway Hill, Weymouth. Following this accident, the bus was returned to Leyland for repair, and continued in the Wilts & Dorset fleet until November 1956. *Brian Jackson collection*

Right: **SALISBURY** This Leyland TS1 coach, MW 8758, entered service with Wilts & Dorset in May 1931, It carried a 32-seat coach body built by Harrington. The Thomas Harrington coach works in Sackville Road, Hove, manufactured elegant and high-quality coach bodies for many years, although production eventually ceased in 1966. A very inviting and attractive vehicle for a coach trip, MW 8758 was photographed in Blue Boar Row, Salisbury, when new. This coach served Wilts & Dorset very well, remaining in the fleet until November 1952, having been rebuilt by Eastern Coach Works in 1944. *David Pennels collection*

Left: **AMESBURY** A bus station at Amesbury came into use in the summer of 1933. It was built by James & Crockerell of Durrington, and was a single-storey building that included a passenger waiting room and local offices as well as a lock-up shop. Awaiting departure time at the new bus station with a service to Andover is MW 8755, a Leyland TD1 carrying a 48-seat lowbridge body, also by Leyland. New to Wilts & Dorset in June 1931, MW 8755 was subsequently rebuilt by Eastern Coach Works in 1946, and after being withdrawn by Wilts & Dorset in 1951 saw further service with Potteries Motor Traction. *David Pennels collection*

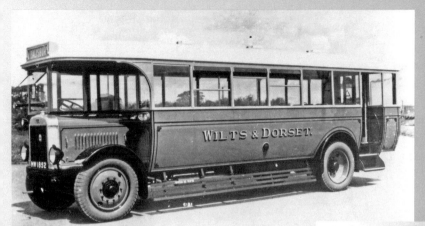

Left: **LEYLAND** Here we see another attractive all-Leyland vehicle. Leyland PLSC3 saloon MW 1852 was new to Wilts & Dorset in May 1928, and this photograph was taken by the manufacturer prior to delivery. Notice the lettering 'speed 12mph'; this was the maximum permitted speed for buses when MW 1852 was new in 1928; it was increased to 30mph by the 1930 Road Traffic Act. Subsequently rebodied by Beadle in 1946, MW 1852 was in service with Wilts & Dorset until July 1950. *David Pennels collection*

Right: **PARK ROYAL** Between October 1937 and June 1939 Wilts & Dorset took delivery of nine Leyland TD5 double-deck buses with 52-seat lowbridge bodies by Park Royal. The long seats on the upper deck, each normally seating four passengers, can be seen in this body-builder's photograph of BAM 51, the first of the batch, which was new to Wilts & Dorset in October 1937. It remained in the Wilts & Dorset fleet until August 1955, its bodywork having been rebuilt by Portsmouth Aviation in 1947. *David Pennels collection*

Wilts & Dorset in wartime

Right: **SALISBURY** At 11.00am on Sunday 3 September 1939 Prime Minister Neville Chamberlain announced that Great Britain was at war with Germany. Petrol rationing began very quickly afterwards, taking effect from midnight on 22 September – meaning that, for the majority of people, anyone who needed or wanted to travel further than walking of cycling distance normally had no other option than to use public transport. The route between Salisbury and Bournemouth via Ringwood and Christchurch was operated jointly by Wilts & Dorset and Hants & Dorset. Representing the latter, Bristol K5G FLJ 534, new in May 1940 and carrying a 53-seat Eastern Coach Works lowbridge body, has just arrived in Salisbury bus station (opened in August 1939) from Bournemouth. A long queue is waiting to board; notice also the 'A' board indicating where intending passengers should queue for buses to Bournemouth. FLJ 534 was is service with Hants & Dorset until August 1959. Wilts & Dorset took delivery of 12 very similar Bristol K5G double-deck buses during the early months of 1940; these were the Company's first Bristol/Eastern Coach Works vehicles – a combination that would become very familiar during the post-war years. *H&DW&D Heritage Collection, courtesy Peter Cook*

Left: **MARLBOROUGH** In wartime guise, complete with masked headlights and white-painted tips to its front mudguards, Leyland TD3 WV 4923 waits at Marlborough, ready to return to Salisbury. Carrying a 52-seat lowbridge body by Brush, this bus entered service with Wilts & Dorset in May 1934; after the war it was rebodied by Willowbrook in 1946, which prolonged its life with the company until January 1955. Blackout conditions made bus work very difficult during the hours of darkness; the problems that were faced by drivers are easy to imagine, but conductors also had their own problems with fare collection in virtually unlit buses. *H&DW&D Heritage Collection, courtesy Peter Cook*

Right: **IRTHLINGBOROUGH** By early 1939 the international situation was such that war seemed inevitable, and this led to a rapid expansion of military facilities on Salisbury Plain and the construction of a large army camp at Blandford. Wilts & Dorset gained the contracts to provide transport for the construction workers involved in building these camps, which required a massive and immediate increase in the size of the fleet. Second-hand buses were sourced from all over the country; Southdown supplied 58 buses, but the example seen here came from neighbouring Hants & Dorset. Leyland TD1 RU 9490 had been new to the Bournemouth-based operator in May 1929, and had passed to Wilts & Dorset in April 1939. In 1943 it was sent to Eastern Coach Works at Irthlingborough, Northamptonshire, where that company had relocated from Lowestoft during the war. It emerged with this new lowbridge body, built in a style that looked forward towards the post-war ECW double-deck body, although such features as the limited number of opening windows (as well as the masked headlights, etc) are a reminder that this was still wartime, despite the body not being as austere as many that were produced during that period. Thus rejuvenated, RU 9490 remained in the Wilts & Dorset fleet until June 1952. *David Pennels collection*

Left: **SALISBURY** In order to reduce dependence on imported oil, the Government requested bus operators to convert 10% of their fleets to run on gas; these buses towed trailers that produced the gas by burning anthracite. The operational performance of these converted buses was very poor, and they were expensive to maintain. Wilts & Dorset converted the route between Salisbury and Wilton to gas operation, but even with a special rota of drivers it was found necessary to add 5 minutes to the schedule for each journey. Complete with TIM ticket machine, a conductress looks from the rear platform of Leyland TD1 UF 7415 in Blue Boar Row, Salisbury, some time during 1944. As its registration number indicates, UF 7415 had been new to Southdown, and was one of the many vehicles acquired by Wilts & Dorset from that undertaking in 1939 and subsequently rebodied. Everyone was pleased when gas propulsion of buses was phased out towards the end of the war, and by advertising in the local press Wilts & Dorset managed to sell off its gas producer trailers for £20 each in 1945. It must also be mentioned that Wilts & Dorset made another vital contribution to the war effort; around 50% of the Company's workshop in Castle Street, Salisbury, was requisitioned for the production of wings and fuselages for Spitfire aircraft. *J. Taylor, David Pennels collection*

Left: **SALISBURY** A year after the end of the war, life was gradually returning to normal, although shortages and rationing would continue for some years to come. Leyland TD1 MW 7050 can be seen on the right in this photograph, taken at Salisbury bus station on 2 July 1946. This bus had entered service in July 1930, and by the time this photograph was taken its 48-seat lowbridge Leyland body had been extensively rebuilt by Eastern Coach Works in 1945, enabling this bus to remain in service with Wilts & Dorset until October 1951. *David Pennels collection*

Right: **SALISBURY** Like every other bus operator, Wilts & Dorset was in urgent need of new buses after the war. The first post-war double-deckers were two Bristol K5Gs with 55-seat lowbridge bodywork by Eastern Coach Works, which arrived in March 1946. These were followed by another three identical vehicles in the early summer of that year. DMR 840 was brand new when it was photographed loading passengers for Woodfalls at Salisbury bus station, also on 2 July 1946. The combination of a Bristol chassis with an Eastern Coach Works body was now the standard for new vehicle purchases. Notice the advertisement for a 'War Office approved tailor' between the decks, as well as the long queue of waiting passengers on the left of the photograph. *David Pennels collection*

Left: **SALISBURY** When Leyland LT1 saloon MW 5800 had entered traffic with Wilts & Dorset in November 1929, it had carried a 31-seat bus body also built by Leyland. At the outbreak of war in 1939 this vehicle had been temporarily converted for use as an ambulance, but in November 1945 it was given a completely new single-deck bus body built in Wilts & Dorset's own workshop, with seats for 32 passengers. The Company was justifiably proud of this new body, and MW 5800 was posed for the camera not long after the work had been completed. It was withdrawn from service in November 1952. *David Pennels collection*

Below: **SALISBURY** A number of the second-hand double-deck buses acquired in 1939 for the Blandford Camp contract went on to give good service to Wilts & Dorset for a considerable time after the war. A good example is UF 7403, a Leyland TD1 that had first entered traffic with Southdown in 1931. When this bus was acquired by Wilts & Dorset in 1939 it still carried its original Short 50-seat highbridge body. This was replaced by a new Willowbrook 51-seat lowbridge body in June 1944, as can be seen in this photograph of the bus awaiting its next call to duty at Salt Lane car park, Salisbury, on 15 March 1953. It was withdrawn from service in October of that year. *David Pennels*

Right: **AMESBURY** Departing from Amesbury bus station on route 3 to Larkhill via Bulford we see AHR 399, a Leyland TD4 with 52-seat Leyland lowbridge bodywork that was in service with Wilts & Dorset from July 1936 until February 1957. The bus station building can be seen in the background; the upper storey was added by James & Crockerell of Durrington at a cost of £2,109 in 1949-50. A letter from the builder, sent to Wilts & Dorset in April 1950, gave assurances that the flat roof had been thoroughly tested by having a number of buckets of water thrown over it, and moreover there had since been three days of almost continuous rain without any water ingress into the new building. The letter concluded that the slight buckling that had been noted in the roofing material was down to the flexible nature of the product used, and was not detrimental to the structure. These buildings at Amesbury, photographed here on 27 September 1953, remained until 1997 when they were demolished to allow the bus station to be reconfigured. *David Pennels*

Left: **SALISBURY** Awaiting departure time outside Style & Gerrish (now Debenham's) in Blue Boar Row, Salisbury, sister bus AHR 400 was likewise new in July 1936. These two Leyland TD4s carried early examples of Leyland's five-bay bodywork; they were pleasing in appearance and their performance was good too, with both seeing more than 20 years in service. In 1949 AHR 400 had been fitted with an experimental form of fluorescent interior lighting; although this equipment was subsequently removed, it is believed to have been one of the first installations of its kind on a bus. This photograph was taken on 13 March 1957; AHR 400 looks in fine condition, but was withdrawn from service later that month. *David Pennels*

Left: **SALISBURY** Salt Lane car park is a mere stone's throw from Salisbury bus station, and during the 1940s and 1950s was used to park buses awaiting the call to duty. Two single-deck buses are seen in this view. On the left by the advertisement hoardings is MW 3851, a Leyland PLSC3 that had been new to Wilts & Dorset in March 1929 and had received a new 32-seat Beadle body in November 1945; this bus was withdrawn in June 1950. On the right, and closer to the camera, is AMW 481, a Leyland LT7 with 32-seat Harrington bodywork, new in March 1937 and withdrawn in January 1956. *David Pennels collection*

Right: **WEYMOUTH** Wilts & Dorset's first new post-war coaches did not enter service until the beginning of the 1949 season, although some of the vehicles had been received the previous year, including EMW 282, which was delivered to the Company in November 1948. Nine Bristol L6B coaches came into use in the spring of 1949, and these attractive and comfortable vehicles served Wilts & Dorset very well. EMW 282 was photographed while on an excursion at Weymouth; this fine vehicle, which carried a 32-seat rear-entrance body by Beadle, was retained on coach duties until withdrawal in September 1961. *R. H. G. Simpson, Brian Jackson collection*

Right: **BASINGSTOKE** From 1926 onwards bus services in the Basingstoke area had been provided by a company called Venture. This undertaking was acquired by Red & White United Transport in 1945, which in turn sold out to the British Transport Commission in 1950. The BTC placed Venture under the control of Wilts & Dorset from 1 January 1951, giving the Company a whole network of routes that went nowhere near either of the two counties mentioned in its title. Some of the buses acquired from Venture continued in the Wilts & Dorset fleet for some time; this photograph was taken in 1961, ten years after the takeover, and on the left shows HAD 745, an AEC Regent III that had formerly been in the Venture fleet. Notice the greater height of the highbridge bodywork carried by this bus when compared with the other vehicles visible in the photograph. Coming towards the camera is Bristol KS6B GMW 194, which had been new to Wilts & Dorset in October 1950 and carries Eastern Coach Works lowbridge bodywork. The helpful conductor places a pushchair onto the pavement in readiness for an alighting passenger. *H&DW&D Heritage Collection, courtesy Peter Cook*

Left: **BASINGSTOKE** Among the more unusual buses acquired by Wilts & Dorset with the Venture concern were two AEC Regal single-deckers that carried 31-seat open-rear-platform bodywork by Park Royal. COT 547 had been new in May 1938, and is seen here on 4 September 1954. It remained in the Wilts & Dorset fleet until February 1956. *David Pennels*

Right: **SALISBURY** Urgent need for additional single-deck buses led to Wilts & Dorset acquiring a number of second-hand vehicles of this type in 1952. BOW 169 had been new to Hants & Dorset in July 1938; it carried a 31-seat Beadle body that had been rebuilt by Hants & Dorset in May 1950. This bus passed to Wilts & Dorset in February 1952, and served as a bus until September 1955, although it was destined to remain with the Company in another capacity for much longer (see also page 35). *H&DW&D Heritage Collection, courtesy Peter Cook*

Left: **MINEHEAD** Wilts & Dorset started to take delivery of underfloor-engined single-deck vehicles in November 1952. These were Bristol LS6Gs with dual-purpose Eastern Coach Works bodies that originally seated 39 passengers. Painted in the Company's coach livery, they were soon put to work on a variety of duties, including excursions and weekend forces leave express services. By October 1953, when JWV 762 entered traffic, Wilts & Dorset had 36 vehicles of this type. As delivered they had featured a front entrance and a rear exit, but within a few years the rear exits had been removed, increasing the seating capacity to 41 passengers. JWV 762 is seen at Minehead, Somerset, while operating an excursion in 1955; the rear exit had been removed in January of that year. *R. H. G. Simpson, Brian Jackson collection*

Right: **WINCHESTER** The former Venture route 11 from Basingstoke to Winchester was renumbered 111 by Wilts & Dorset. Running via Dummer, North Waltham, Popham and Lunways Inn, the route traversed sparsely populated countryside and also had to compete with a faster end-to-end rail service. Nonetheless a number of passengers can be seen on board EJB 521, photographed at Winchester bus station on 27 June 1953. This AEC Regent III carried Weymann/Lydney highbridge bodywork seating 56 passengers. It had entered service with Newbury & District in 1948 and was transferred to Wilts & Dorset at Basingstoke in January 1951. It was in service with Wilts & Dorset until September 1962. *David Pennels*

Left: **BASINGSTOKE** The final batches of lowbridge buses delivered to Wilts & Dorset featured a modification in the design of the upstairs seating in that each bench seat now consisted of four slightly staggered individual seats. This ensured that upper-deck passengers sat four across rather than each bench seat accommodating three very well-spaced and comfortable people who would only very reluctantly move up to admit a fourth if the bus was absolutely full. Most of Wilts & Dorset's buses of this revised design were Bristol KSW6Bs, but there were four KSW5Gs, including JMW 955, new in August 1953 and seen here on 10 September 1955. The Barge Inn was the main terminal point in Basingstoke during the 1950s, and the bus station was subsequently built in that location. *David Pennels*

Right: **SALISBURY** During the Second World War, such new buses that were available after the end of 1940 were built to Ministry of Supply austerity specifications and were allocated by the Government to operators with little regard to chassis make, etc. Thus it was that in 1943 Wilts & Dorset was allocated four Daimler CWG5s carrying 55-seat lowbridge bodywork by Brush. These new buses were soon allocated to the long Salisbury-Blandford-Weymouth route. The bodies were rebuilt by Wilts & Dorset after the war to conform more to peacetime standards, and the Daimlers saw more employment on some of the Company's longer routes, being frequently allocated on journeys from Salisbury to Southampton and occasionally to Bournemouth. From around 1953 onwards they ended their days mostly on Salisbury city services, as exemplified by CWV 779, caught by the camera on route 60 to Wilton. This bus was withdrawn from service in October 1957. *David Pennels*

Left: **SALISBURY** Because of restricted height clearances on a number of routes, for many years most of Wilts & Dorset's double-deck buses had been of the lowbridge type, with a sunken side gangway on the upper deck. This arrangement had a number of disadvantages, so when Bristol and Eastern Coach Works introduced the Lodekka in the early 1950s, producing a bus with a centre gangway on both decks within a similar height to the old lowbridge type, this new development was widely welcomed. Wilts & Dorset received its first batch of three Lodekkas in March 1954. One of the trio was KMR 609, a Bristol LD6G seen here at Salisbury garage when newly delivered. With seats for 58 passengers, these first examples were put to work on Salisbury city services (see also page 37). *H&DW&D Heritage Collection, courtesy Peter Cook*

Left: **SALISBURY** Although Wilts & Dorset had started taking delivery of underfloor-engined single-deck vehicles from late 1952, the Company considered that the traditional half-cab single-deck bus was more suited to the rough roads then to be found on some of the more rural routes. Accordingly during October and November 1954 a batch of 15 Bristol LWL5Gs with 39-seat rear-entrance bodywork by Eastern Coach Works was built as a special order for Wilts & Dorset – by then this layout was considered obsolete for single-deck buses. Nonetheless, as built these were certainly attractive vehicles, as shown by LAM 744, new in October 1954 and seen here in Salisbury bus station on 4 April 1956, having arrived from Shaftesbury on route 29 via Bowerchalke and Broad Chalke. *David Pennels*

Right: **SALISBURY** The design of these 15 single-deck buses meant that they required a crew of two – driver and conductor – to run in service, and by the late 1950s the economics of rural bus operation were such that driver-only operation was becoming vital if the network was to be sustained. In July 1958 LAM 744 was returned to Eastern Coach Works where it was rebuilt with a forward entrance, and a small area for a ticket machine was created at the nearside rear of the cab. Thus modified, LAM 744 was photographed at Salisbury bus station ready to depart for Great Durnford in the Woodford valley on route 1. *David Pennels*

Left: **SALISBURY** Drivers considered that the layout of LAM 744 after conversion was unworkable, so it was soon decided to give the rest of the vehicles in this batch a more extensive rebuild in Wilts & Dorset's own workshop. As well as being converted to forward entrance, the buses were given a full front with much of the front bulkhead being removed, allowing the sound of the Gardner 5LW engine to reverberate around the saloon. The look of these buses was changed considerably, as illustrated by KWV 934, new in October 1954, rebuilt by Wilts & Dorset in November 1959, and caught by the camera ready to depart from Salisbury bus station for Shaftesbury. These rebuilt buses were called 'conkerboxes' by the staff and were used widely across the Company's network during the 1960s. The original Eastern Coach Works conversion – LAM 744 – was similarly rebuilt by Wilts & Dorset in March 1960. *Brian Jackson collection*

Right: **AMESBURY** Two of the Company's older buses are among those parked at Amesbury on 1 May 1954. On the left we see Leyland TD4 WV 7474, which had been involved in an unfortunate incident while running from Salisbury to Weymouth in 1935 (see page 7). The saloon just visible on the right is EEL 800, a Bristol L5G that had been new to Hants & Dorset in August 1938; transferred to Wilts & Dorset in March 1952, it was withdrawn from service in October 1954. *David Pennels*

Left: **BASINGSTOKE** AEC Regal FOT 204, carrying a 32-seat forward-entrance body by Duple, had been new to Venture in April 1947 and came to Wilts & Dorset in January 1951. It was used as a dual-purpose vehicle until the body was rebuilt by Wilts & Dorset in January 1955, and thereafter was used almost exclusively on bus work. In this photograph it is parked at Basingstoke having recently operated a journey on route 117. This ran on Wednesdays and Saturdays only from Hartley Wespall to Basingstoke via Lyde Green and Newnham Green. FOT 204 was withdrawn in September 1961. *H&DW&D Heritage Collection, courtesy Peter Cook*

Right: **PEWSEY** Also acquired with the Venture operation at Basingstoke in 1951 were two Bedford OB saloons, FOR 633 and FOR 634, which dated from 1947. By the time this photograph was taken on 7 July 1954 both of them had been cascaded to Pewsey depot. Seen marked up ready to operate on the 18 route – which ran between Upavon village and RAF Upavon with a journey time of 7 minutes – FOR 633 was caught by the camera basking in the sunshine at Frog Meadow, Pewsey depot. *David Pennels*

Left: **SALISBURY** In the early months of the Second World War Wilts & Dorset was fortunate to take delivery of a batch of 12 Bristol K5G double-deck buses carrying 52-seat lowbridge bodywork by Eastern Coach Works. These had been the first Bristol/ECW buses to enter the Wilts & Dorset fleet, and they had been built to full peacetime standards. Rugged and reliable, these fine buses gave the Company yeoman service for many years. Two members of the batch were caught by the camera at Salt Lane car park in Salisbury towards the end of their service with the Company, and by then in rebuilt form; closest to the camera is CHR 498 and next to it CHR 497. Both buses had been new in January 1940; CHR 498 was withdrawn by Wilts & Dorset in October 1959 and later saw further service with the Esso Petroleum Company at Fawley Refinery, while CHR 497 was taken out of service in August 1959. *Brian Jackson collection*

Right: **DURRINGTON** The Wilts & Dorset 5 route ran from Marlborough to Salisbury via Oare, Pewsey, Upavon, Netheravon, Durrington and Amesbury; in terms of passenger loadings it was a busier route between Marlborough and Salisbury than the 9, which ran via Burbage, Tidworth and the Bourne Valley. Operating the 5 route on 26 May 1957, the Pewsey depot driver in charge of HMR 688 is negotiating Charlie's Corner at Durrington with some verve while on the way to Salisbury. This bus is a Bristol KSW5G with a 55-seat lowbridge Eastern Coach Works body, and had been new to Wilts & Dorset in February 1952. *David Pennels*

Left: **TUNBRIDGE WELLS** Early in 1958 Wilts & Dorset introduced a new coach livery comprising red below the waist and cream above, as illustrated by GAM 214, photographed while operating an excursion – driver Jack Warrilow stands proudly with his repainted vehicle during a layover at the tour destination on 2 July 1958. This Bristol L6B, carrying a 32-seat coach body by Portsmouth Aviation, had been new to Wilts & Dorset in 1950, and the body had been rebuilt by the Company in January 1958; it remained in the fleet until September 1961. *David Pennels*

Right: **SALISBURY** Industrial unrest affected the bus industry during the summer of 1957. From midnight on 19 July bus staff in most areas of the country came out on strike in pursuit of a pay claim for an additional £1 (20 shillings) per week – the employers had offered only 3 shillings. The dispute was referred to arbitration, and a revised offer of an additional 11 shillings per week made on 26 July was accepted, and the bus crews returned to work. Salisbury bus station looks strangely empty when photographed during the dispute on 20 July 1957. *David Pennels*

Left: **ANDOVER** The Wilts & Dorset 69 route was a local service linking Andover Guildhall and Hedge End Road, a short trip that was allowed 6 minutes for the outward journey and 5 for the return. Bristol KSW5G HAM 230, new in September 1951, was photographed on a journey from Hedge End Road to the Guildhall. The 55-seat Eastern Coach Works lowbridge body provided ample accommodation for the passengers using the service. *H&DW&D Heritage Collection, courtesy Peter Cook*

Right: **NEWBURY** One of a batch of five similar vehicles, Bristol KS6B GMW 195 was first licensed by Wilts & Dorset in January 1951 and was put to work on former Venture routes in Basingstoke. Eight years later, on 31 January 1959, this bus was caught by the camera at The Wharf in Newbury while operating on route 135 to Whitway. A few journeys on the 135 route continued onwards from Whitway to Whitchurch, and offered connections with King Alfred buses to and from Winchester. *David Pennels*

Left: **SALISBURY** The summer of 1959 was notably warm and sunny, and the open windows on Bristol LD6G SHR 440, seen here in New Canal, Salisbury, on 3 June will be noted. Notice also that all of the side windows on this vehicle, which had been new the previous year, are of the hopper rather than the sliding type. The ornate building visible at the rear of the bus is a cinema; at the time of this photograph it was called the Gaumont. The outer foyer dates back to 1740, although the Tudor-style facade was designed by Pugin and added in 1834. It became a cinema when the auditorium was built in 1931. Subsequently it was renamed the Odeon in 1964, and the auditorium is now divided into several screens, as is the modern practice, but pleasingly the listed frontage and foyer remain. *David Pennels*

Right: **AMESBURY** When photographed at Amesbury, Bristol LD6B NHR 909 had been operating the short but busy run to Boscombe Down on route 7. This bus was one of three that had been new in 1956, originally allocated to Blandford depot and used on the Salisbury-Blandford-Weymouth route; they remained at Blandford until this route was converted to driver-only operation in October 1959. In its new location, NHR 909 would have plenty of passengers to carry to Boscombe Down. *H&DW&D Heritage Collection, courtesy Peter Cook*

Left: **SALISBURY** Delivered to Wilts & Dorset in December 1953 and entering traffic in January 1954, KHR 530 was one of a batch of Bristol KSW6Bs fitted with manually operated platform doors and intended for longer-distance routes. Appropriately it was awaiting departure time for Zeals on route 25 when this photograph was taken in Salisbury bus station on 27 May 1961. Complete with Clayton heaters, these KSW6Bs were very pleasant vehicles in which to enjoy a journey at any time of year. *David Pennels*

Right: **SALISBURY** New in July 1961, XMR 947 was a Bristol MW6G coach with seats for 39 passengers in its Eastern Coach Works body. In 1962 is was repainted into Wilts & Dorset's new predominantly cream coach livery, as seen in this view taken at Salisbury garage. Day trips by coach were an important part of the business in the early 1960s and the tours and excursions programme for 1962 included such delights as Lynton & Lynmouth, Worcester & The Malvern Hills, Seaton, a conducted tour of London Airport, and even special day trips to the Channel Islands (travelling by ship from Weymouth). *H&DW&D Heritage Collection, courtesy Peter Cook*

Left: **BASINGSTOKE** Wilts & Dorset opened a new bus station and garage at Basingstoke on 28 June 1962. In what is clearly a posed photograph, the garage area can be seen immediately prior to opening. A former Venture AEC double-deck bus and a Bristol LS saloon can be seen through the open doorway, while a lowbridge Bristol KSW double-decker is over the furthest pit on the left. Tobacco was still freely advertised at that time, and it can be seen that Nelson cigarettes cost 3s 10d for 20 in the summer of 1962. Some of the departure stands in the new bus station can also be glimpsed through the open doorway. *The late C. J. Burt collection*

Right: **BOURNEMOUTH** The unusual two-tier bus and coach station in Exeter Road, Bournemouth, was completely rebuilt between 1957 and 1959. With green Hants & Dorset buses visible in the background, Wilts & Dorset Bristol LD6G OHR 124, new in November 1956, is seen departing on route 38 to Salisbury via Christchurch, Ringwood and Fordingbridge. The 38 was operated jointly by Wilts & Dorset and Hants & Dorset. *H&DW&D Heritage Collection, courtesy Peter Cook*

Left: **KNIGHTON** None of us who experienced it will ever forget the 1962-63 winter. Christmas 1962 was a very seasonable one, with snow in many areas on Boxing Day. This was just a foretaste of what was to come; during the early hours of Sunday 30 December a blizzard blanketed Southern England in deep snow, with strong winds causing considerable drifting. The following day Bristol LS6G dual-purpose saloon JMR 323 set out from Salisbury bound for Netheravon on route 5, but became stuck in a snowdrift near Knighton between Hackthorn and the Figheldean turning on the A 345. The blizzard was followed by almost eight weeks when the daytime temperature rarely rose above freezing point and the nights were bitterly cold, a minimum of zero Fahrenheit being recorded on one occasion, and conditions were not helped by further snowfall and freezing rain. Nonetheless, every effort was made to provide the best service possible in what were really appalling conditions. The last of the snow did not melt until early March 1963. *David Pennels*

Right: **SALISBURY** The operations of Silver Star, a bus and coach company based at Porton Down and founded by Eddie Shergold and Ben White in 1923, were taken over by Wilts & Dorset on 5 June 1963. At that time Silver Star had 23 vehicles; Wilts & Dorset retained nine of them and the others went to various fleets including Western National and Bristol Omnibus Company. One of the Silver Star vehicles retained by Wilts & Dorset was PHR 829, a Leyland Tiger Cub that had been new in 1957. Photographed at Salisbury bus station on 6 June 1963, it is departing on a trip to Porton Camp, a route on which it was often used by Silver Star. At this juncture PHR 829 was still in Silver Star colours with just the former fleet names obliterated, but these acquired vehicles were soon repainted in Wilts & Dorset livery. *David Pennels*

Left: **SALISBURY** The first two forward-entrance double-deck buses in the Wilts & Dorset fleet entered service in 1963. Bristol FLF6G 467 BMR was photographed at Salisbury bus station after arriving from Bournemouth on route 38. The Eastern Coach Works body had seats for 70 passengers, but these two FLFs were the final two Wilts & Dorset double-deckers to feature the comfortable camel-back semi-coach seating that the Company had specified as a standard since November 1957 (see also page 32). This vehicle may have generated some interest among passengers at Bournemouth; Hants & Dorset did not get any forward-entrance FLF double-deckers until early 1965. *R. H. G. Simpson, Brian Jackson collection*

Right: **SALISBURY** Among the new vehicles delivered to Wilts & Dorset in 1964 were eight Bristol FS6B double-deck buses with 60-seat rear-entrance bodies by Eastern Coach Works. Exemplifying this batch of buses, 478 BMR is seen in New Canal while working an afternoon journey on route 24 from Salisbury to Trowbridge. *H&DW&D Heritage Collection, courtesy Peter Cook*

Left: **SALISBURY** Four Bristol FLF6Gs also joined the Wilts & Dorset fleet in 1964; AHR 244B was photographed in absolutely pristine condition in Salisbury works immediately after delivery from Eastern Coach Works on 15 August. Comparison of this photograph with that of 467 BMR on the opposite page illustrates the return to standard bus-type seating on AHR 244B. Crews tended to have mixed feelings about the FLFs; some liked them but others preferred the traditional rear-platform-type bus for operation with a driver and conductor. *David Pennels*

Right: **SALISBURY** April 1966 was unseasonably cool, and in the days following Easter parts of Southern England received a considerable snowfall, although fortunately this only lasted for a couple of days. The bus services were able to keep running, and here we see a rather snow-encrusted Bristol LS saloon ready to depart for a route 5 journey to Upavon, Pewsey and Marlborough on 14 April. To the left of the photograph a similar Bristol LS saloon has been marked up for the relatively short journey on route 56 to Netherhampton, while the Bristol Lodekka in the left background will run on route 8 to Andover via Tidworth. *David Pennels*

Left: **SALISBURY** The new limited-stop service 38A between Salisbury and Bournemouth started on 31 January 1966. It ran on Mondays to Saturdays, and there were two journeys per day in each direction, with timings arranged to be especially suitable for commuters to Bournemouth and day visitors to Salisbury. Running via Fordingbridge, Ringwood, Ferndown, Parley Cross and Winton, the journey time from Salisbury to Bournemouth was 78 minutes. When introduced, journeys on the 38A were normally operated by Bristol FS6G 684 AAM, which was painted in a special cream livery for this purpose. It is seen at Salisbury bus station on a summer evening in 1967, departing for the garage after arrival with the 17.35 journey from Bournemouth. Notice the prominent Bus Station sign and the clock on the corner of the building. *Omnicolour*

Right: **SALISBURY** Passengers travelling on the 38A enjoyed a comfortable journey in the camel-back semi-coach seats fitted to 1962 Bristol FS6G 684 AAM. Similar comfort could also be enjoyed on many other Wilts & Dorset routes during the 1960s, as this type of seating was a standard feature in new Wilts & Dorset buses placed in service between 1957 and 1963. Here we see the interior of the upper deck of 687 AAM, a Bristol FS from 1962 carrying an identical body to that of 684 AAM. *David Pennels*

Left: **CHICHESTER** Acquired with the Silver Star business in 1963, WWV 564 was a Leyland Leopard L2 with a 41-seat Harrington coach body that had been new in 1960. When this photograph was taken on 5 May 1968 it was still very much a front-line coach with Wilts & Dorset, and on this occasion has been hired for a Sunday trip by the Salisbury Bus Enthusiasts group. *David Pennels*

Right: **SALISBURY** It was very unfortunate that a vehicle ran into the rear of WWV 564 in 1970, as being by then ten years old it was not repaired as a coach; however, Wilts & Dorset's skilled engineers rebuilt it as a useful driver-only-operated bus. The limited stop 38A route had been converted to driver-only operation by the end of the 1960s, and WWV 564 is seen in Salisbury bus station picking up passengers for Bournemouth on 30 July 1971. *David Pennels*

Above: **SOUTHSEA** Five dual-purpose Bristol MW6G saloons received by Wilts & Dorset in 1966 were used on a variety of work, including relief journeys for Royal Blue express services, private hire and excursions and tours. The first of the quintet, EMR 302D, is seen in the centre of this picture while laying over after operating the outward journey on an excursion to Southsea. On the left, 3850 R is a Ford 507E coach that had been new in 1963 to Pebley Beach of Wroughton and passed to Rimes of Swindon in 1965, while on the right 470 FCG is an AEC Reliance 4MU4RA carrying 49-seat Park Royal bodywork, new to Aldershot & District Traction Company in 1963. *Omnicolour*

Right: **NORTH EAST ENGLAND** Even in the late 1960s weekend forces leave express coach services from the Salisbury Plain camps were still a considerable operation, with coaches running to various parts of the country – outward on a Friday evening and returning on Sunday. Rather than have the coach stand idle at the distant location on the Saturday, it and the driver were often hired to the transport operator in that area. In this photograph Duple-bodied Bedford VAL70, LMR 734F, bought new by Wilts & Dorset in 1968, is carrying holidaymakers from Newcastle-upon-Tyne to Bridlington while operating on hire to United Automobile Services. *David Pennels collection*

BASINGSTOKE The upper photograph on page 17 illustrates Bristol L5G saloon BOW 169 at Salisbury garage shortly after that 1938-built vehicle was acquired from Hants & Dorset in 1952. After being withdrawn as a bus by Wilts & Dorset in 1955, it was converted by the Company into a breakdown recovery vehicle, entering service in that capacity in January 1956. It was caught by the camera at Basingstoke in the late 1960s complete with trade plate 142 MR. *Brian Jackson collection*

LONDON Passengers travelling on the Royal Blue relief coach to London on this occasion in 1971 probably rubbed their eyes when they saw the vehicle provided. Originally a Bristol L6G, KEL 408 had been new to Hants & Dorset in July 1950 carrying a 28-seat Portsmouth Aviation coach body. In 1961 the coach body was removed, the chassis was lengthened to 30 feet and a six-cylinder Bristol AVW engine fitted; it was then fitted with a new Eastern Coach Works 39-seat bus body, and re-entered service with Hants & Dorset as a driver-only-operated Bristol LL6B bus in April 1962. The engine was still at the front beside the driver, and the noise level inside the saloon was considerable. KEL 408 passed to Wilts & Dorset in August 1970, and was normally used on rather more local duties. Nonetheless, this by then elderly vehicle was still capable of spirited running – apparently it overtook the service coach and beat it into London's Victoria coach station by a comfortable margin. This was, however, something of a swansong for KEL 408; it was withdrawn in July 1972. *Brian Jackson*

WINCHESTER Wilts & Dorset received its first Bristol RE saloons early in 1969, and MMW 352G from this batch was photographed in Andover Road, Winchester, on service 68 – a route that was operated jointly by Wilts & Dorset and Hants & Dorset. Management of the Wilts & Dorset and Hants & Dorset undertakings had been merged in 1964, and these first RE saloons were the final new buses for Wilts & Dorset to carry the familiar Wiltshire registrations; new vehicles joining the fleet after April 1969 were registered in Bournemouth. *H&DW&D Heritage Collection, courtesy Peter Cook*

The Hants & Dorset years

MARLBOROUGH Boasting the second widest High Street in England (the widest is at Stockton-on-Tees), Marlborough was for many years an important interchange point for bus services, as illustrated in this 1974 photograph. Bristol MW6G XMR 942, new as a coach in 1961 but now converted for use as a driver-only-operated bus, has arrived from Salisbury on route 205, while Bristol Omnibus Company RE THU 346G is ready to depart for Hungerford – the latter's driver takes the opportunity to chat with the driver of the 205 as he awaits departure time. Notice Woolworth's shop in the background – another once familiar name that has vanished from our High Streets. *Brian Jackson*

BASINGSTOKE It was announced by the National Bus Company that from October 1972 Wilts & Dorset would be completely absorbed into Hants & Dorset, with all buses running under the latter name. As repaints became due, the buses would be given NBC poppy red livery – lighter than the red previously used by Wilts & Dorset and a radical change from the former Hants & Dorset green livery. Local bus services in Winchester had for many years been operated by King Alfred Motor Services, a company owned by the Chisnell brothers, who by 1973 wished to retire. A long route operated by King Alfred was its service 11 from Winchester to Basingstoke via Whitchurch and Sutton Scotney. Standing out among the red-liveried Bristol/Eastern Coach Works buses, a King Alfred Leyland Atlantean was photographed at Basingstoke bus station on 18 April 1973. Ten days later, Saturday 28 April, was the last day of operation for King Alfred buses, the routes thereafter being operated by Hants & Dorset; the Leyland Atlantean seen here was one of the former King Alfred vehicles that was taken into Hants & Dorset stock. *David Pennels*

SALISBURY Newly repainted in National Bus Company poppy red livery, and with the Hants & Dorset fleet name, Bristol LD6G KMR 609 was caught by the camera waiting to depart from Salisbury centre for Bemerton Heath on 13 July 1973. This bus had entered traffic on Salisbury city routes in March 1954 (see page 19) and was still looking splendid while operating in the same group of services more than 19 years later. *David Pennels*

BEMERTON A problem that faced the Company during the early and middle 1970s was the long delay in the delivery of new buses. Accordingly vehicles were moved around the various depots in order to make the best use of existing stock. Bristol MW5G saloon XEL 551 had been new to Hants & Dorset in December 1958. In this 1973 photograph the blue and grey code discs below the fleet number show that it is now allocated to Pewsey depot, although it still wears Hants & Dorset green livery. At that time it was not unusual to see green-liveried buses working on the erstwhile Wilts & Dorset routes. XEL 551 was withdrawn from service in 1974. *David Pennels*

SALISBURY Late in 1973 Hants & Dorset acquired four Leyland PSU3/3RT coaches that had formerly been in the Southdown fleet. 160 AUF had been new to Southdown in 1962, and before entry into service with Hants & Dorset it was repainted into National Bus Company 'local coach' or dual-purpose livery, which actually suited rather well the distinctive Weymann Castillian body with its high curved waist rail. While in service with Hants & Dorset these four coaches were used mainly on local private hire work. When this photograph was taken on 22 January 1977, AUF 160 had been hired by Salisbury Bus Enthusiasts for their 10th anniversary tour – pity the weather wasn't a good deal better! Notice the group's sign in the windscreen. *David Pennels*

Right: **BASINGSTOKE** The Company's vehicle situation was not helped by two serious fires that took place at Basingstoke in September and December 1974. Among the vehicles destroyed in the fire on 21 September were two Leyland National saloons, NEL 852M and NEL 858M, which had only entered service the previous year. Both of these almost new vehicles were beyond repair and had to be withdrawn. *David Pennels*

Left: **SALISBURY** Further purchases of second-hand buses in 1974 included four Bristol FSF6B double-deckers that had started life in the Brighton, Hove & District fleet and which came to Hants & Dorset via Southdown. Seen in Endless Street, Salisbury, ready to depart for Bishopdown by route 262 on 27 October 1975, WNJ 36 had first entered traffic at Brighton in 1962. Notice the Woolpack Inn on the left; Wilts & Dorset had established offices and a passenger waiting room on this site – 6 Endless Street – from February 1930, but seven years later agreement was reached with the brewery Gibbs Mew & Company to exchange its existing Woolpack Inn at 8 Endless Street for this building next door at number 6. Wilts & Dorset must be unique among bus operators in being able to say that it has moved a public house. This swap of premises allowed the demolition of the former Woolpack Inn, which in turn allowed the construction of Salisbury bus station (opened in August 1939) to proceed. *David Pennels*

Right: **HINDON** A photograph of Hindon outstation in the early 1980s shows a line-up of vehicles awaiting the call to duty. On the left is Bristol VR JJT 438N, new in June 1975, while inside the garage are three Leyland National saloons. GLJ 680N, on the left, has dual-purpose bodywork with 48 very comfortable coach seats; it entered service in January 1975 and has white-top dual-purpose livery. MLJ 921P (centre), new in April 1976, and FPR 61V, new in January 1980, are both standard bus-type Leyland Nationals with seats for 49 passengers. The Wiltsway vinyls carried by two of the vehicles refer to the revised bus networks introduced in Wiltshire as a result of the Market Analysis Project (MAP). *Brian Jackson*

Left: **SALISBURY** New to Hants & Dorset in 1975, NJT 33P was a dual-purpose Bristol VR fitted with semi-coach seats. It was photographed at Salisbury bus station on 11 March 1981 while picking up passengers for the 209 route to Andover. The Antonbus vinyls show that this bus was allocated to Andover depot. In the autumn of 1982 the National Bus Company decided that Hants & Dorset would be divided into smaller units with effect from April 1983; the former Wilts & Dorset depots at Andover and Basingstoke would become part of the new Hampshire Bus Company, whilst Salisbury would now be linked with the Hants & Dorset depots at Poole, Lymington and Swanage as the new Wilts & Dorset Bus Company. We will follow the story of the 'new' Wilts & Dorset in the next chapter. *John Weager*

The Wilts & Dorset Bus Company

Right: **BOURNEMOUTH** The first new buses to be placed in service by the Wilts & Dorset Bus Company established in April 1983 were five Leyland Olympian double-deckers with 70-seat dual-purpose bodies by Eastern Coach Works. Appropriately, when delivered these vehicles carried the later version of the National Bus Company 'local coach' livery. New in March 1984, A904 JPR was photographed in Bournemouth Square during the summer of that year while operating a route X3 journey from Bournemouth to Salisbury. *Omnicolour*

Left: **WEYMOUTH** The year 1985 marked 70 years since the formation of Wilts & Dorset Motor Services in 1915, and to celebrate this anniversary the Wilts & Dorset Bus Company repainted a dual-purpose Bristol RE saloon into a special livery. NLJ 871G had been new to Hants & Dorset in April 1969, and certainly looked quite eye-catching in the anniversary livery. Thus adorned, it was used both on ordinary service work and for special events and hires during 1985; here it was caught by the camera at Weymouth. *Brian Jackson*

Below: **LOWER WOODFORD** When Wilts & Dorset started running buses in 1915, the first route was between Amesbury and Salisbury via the Woodford valley. Appropriately, this route always carried service number 1 in the days of Wilts & Dorset Motor Services. During the 1970s it had become the 201 when Hants & Dorset added 200 to all of the former Wilts & Dorset route numbers, but by the time this photograph was taken in the late 1980s the Wilts & Dorset Bus Company had restored it as service 1. The Leyland National seen here, MAR 781P, passing The Wheatsheaf Inn, Lower Woodford, while heading for Salisbury had been new to Eastern National in June 1976; it was acquired by Wilts & Dorset in 1986 and passed to Maidstone & District in August 1992. *The late C. J. Burt collection*

Above: **SALISBURY The** Wilts & Dorset Bus Company was privatised in June 1987, being sold to its local management team. A new livery – still using red as the main colour – and new logo were quickly designed. In August 1993 the Company placed in service a batch of six Optare Delta single-deck buses that were to remain unique in the fleet, as subsequent orders for full-size single-deck buses specified the Optare Excel. Caught by the camera in Bridge Street, Salisbury, in 1994, Optare Delta L506 AJT was operating on route 51 to Bemerton Heath. *Dave Bailey*

Right: **LUDGERSHALL** Ten new double-deck Optare Spectra buses entered service with Wilts & Dorset in April 1993, and became the Company's standard purchase for new double-deckers for the next few years. K108 VLJ from the first batch is seen passing through Ludgershall in 1994 while operating on route 9 from Andover to Salisbury. These smart, modern vehicles did much to enhance the image of the Wilts & Dorset Bus Company. *Dave Bailey*

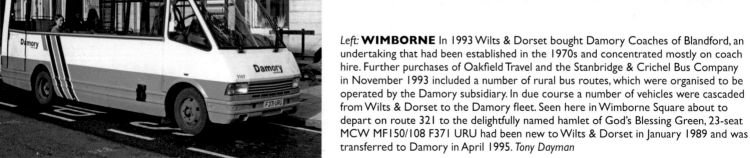

Left: **WIMBORNE** In 1993 Wilts & Dorset bought Damory Coaches of Blandford, an undertaking that had been established in the 1970s and concentrated mostly on coach hire. Further purchases of Oakfield Travel and the Stanbridge & Crichel Bus Company in November 1993 included a number of rural bus routes, which were organised to be operated by the Damory subsidiary. In due course a number of vehicles were cascaded from Wilts & Dorset to the Damory fleet. Seen here in Wimborne Square about to depart on route 321 to the delightfully named hamlet of God's Blessing Green, 23-seat MCW MF150/108 F371 URU had been new to Wilts & Dorset in January 1989 and was transferred to Damory in April 1995. *Tony Dayman*

Left: **STRATFORD SUB CASTLE** Four Optare Spectra double-deck buses delivered early in 1995 were fitted with 73 comfortable semi-coach seats and were painted in Wilts & Dorset's coach livery. As well as operating on some of the longer-distance routes, these vehicles were regularly used for private hire, especially for school groups. Seen almost brand new on 13 February 1995, M138 KRU is picking up pupils from Leaden Hall School outside St Lawrence's Church, Stratford sub Castle. *Richard Weaver*

Right: **STRATFORD BRIDGE** The origins of Tourist Coaches went back prior to the 1920s when a bus service was established by a Mr Stanfield, and the business remained in the ownership of the same family until 1982. It then passed to Mr R. J. Chalk, who in turn sold it to Wilts & Dorset early in 1995, which maintained it as a separate brand, concentrating on coach hire. Two of the vehicles acquired with the Tourist undertaking were photographed at Stratford Bridge in February 1995; B873 XWR is a Volvo B10M dating from May 1985 and carrying 53-seat Plaxton bodywork, while the small coach on the right is a Toyota HB31R with 18-seat Caetano Optimo bodywork, and dates from June 1989. *Richard Weaver*

Right: **SALISBURY** The Optare Solo easy-access single-deck bus was first unveiled at the Bus & Coach Show at the National Exhibition Centre, Birmingham, in October 1997. Wilts & Dorset's directors had worked closely with Optare in the development of the Solo, and the first of these vehicles entered service on the route between Poole and Canford Heath in May 1998. The major launch took place in Salisbury Market Square on Wednesday 26 August 1998, as photographed here, with 16 Optare Solos and three low-floor Optare Spectras arranged for public inspection during that morning. From the following weekend all Salisbury city services were operated by low-floor buses, making Salisbury the first place in the country to achieve a city-wide network of easy-access bus services. *Richard Weaver*

Salisbury Reds

Left: **SALISBURY** Ownership of Wilts & Dorset passed to the Go-Ahead Group in August 2003. Within that group, the individual operating companies are given a high degree of autonomy, while local identities are valued and encouraged. From March 2010 buses on Salisbury city routes were branded as Salisbury Reds; a couple of years later this branding was extended to all bus routes in the Salisbury region (with the exception of the X3 – see the next page). There has been very significant investment in new vehicles, and a batch of Alexander Dennis Enviro 400 double-deckers saw the Salisbury Reds image refreshed with a deeper all-over red livery and a new-style fleet name. Seen in Salisbury bus station in the autumn of 2013, HJ63 JKF is branded for the X5 route to Pewsey, Marlborough and Swindon. *Peter Cook*

Left: **SALISBURY** Built for the requirements of a rather different era, the bus station at Salisbury was 74 years old in 2013, and this ageing structure no longer provided satisfactory accommodation for either customers or staff. It was a logical step to transfer longer-distance services to terminate at city centre stops, just as local routes had done for many years. Accordingly, Saturday 4 January 2014 was the last day that timetabled service buses used the bus station. The last service bus departure of all was the X3 journey to Ringwood at 10 past midnight; Alexander Dennis Enviro 400 HJ63 JJY is seen pulling into Endless Street for the final time, with Ringwood driver Will Degan at the wheel. The bus is in More livery; the Company's services operated in the Poole, Ringwood and Lymington areas now carry the More branding, which was first established in the Poole and Bournemouth area in December 2004. *Brian Jackson*

Right: **AMESBURY** The bus station at Amesbury, opened in 1933 and completely remodelled in 1997, was also closed after operations on Saturday 4 January 2014. Representing Salisbury Reds on the Activ8 route between Andover and Salisbury, operated jointly with Stagecoach, an Alexander Dennis Enviro 400 awaits departure time during the afternoon of the final day of operation for the premises. From the following day services used nearby bus stops instead of calling at the bus station. *Brian Jackson*

Right: **READING** Wilts & Dorset acquired Lever's Coaches of Fovant in 1997, Kingston Coaches in 1998 and Bell's Coaches of Winterslow in 1999. From 2008 onwards, all of the coaches operated by Go South Coast's mainland subsidiaries were painted in a blue livery, with the appropriate fleet name – as demonstrated by YN05 ATY, an Irisbus Eurorider 397E with a 53-seat Beulas body photographed at Reading carrying the Bell's Coaches fleet name. The 'stylish coach hire' strapline is carried by all of the blue-liveried coaches operated by Go South Coast. *David Pennels*

Below right: **SALISBURY** To mark the centenary of Wilts & Dorset in 2015, two buses from the current fleet were repainted into liveries that had been carried in days gone by. On Sunday 14 June 2015 the Company hosted a 100th birthday celebration with an event that included preserved heritage buses offering free rides on a variety of routes from Salisbury city centre. Early that morning ancient and modern were seen together in Blue Boar Row as Scania/East Lancashire Omnidekka YN06 JWX, repainted in 1950s livery and operating on route r1 between Bemerton Heath and Salisbury District Hospital, overtook preserved Bristol KSW HWV 294.

But pleasant as it is to remember the past, it is of vital importance to look to the future. We can be certain that as times continue to change, so the bus industry will continue to face new challenges. There are certainly some encouraging signs; since acquiring Wilts & Dorset in 2003, the Go-Ahead Group has invested significantly in new vehicles and new technology, and the numbers of people choosing to travel by bus have started to grow in several urban areas, although many rural routes have declined. When compared to those featured in the early years covered by this book, today's buses look very different, but one thing has not changed – the cheerful, helpful and friendly service offered to customers – and this should ensure that bus services in the area have a great future. *Brian Jackson*

Index

OARE A reminder of the days when the Company also provided a parcels-by-bus service, this Wilts & Dorset parcel agency sign on the wall of the White Hart at Oare still survives in the 21st century, and was photographed on 10 June 2014. *Brian Jackson*

SALISBURY A top deck view of a lowbridge Bristol KSW, a type operated by Wits & Dorset from the early 1950s until April 1974. *Brian Jackson*